Ethernet Pocket Guide:

A Practical Guide to
Designing, Installing, and Troubleshooting
Ethernet Networks

Ethernet Pocket Guide

A Practical Guide to Designing,

Installing, and Troubleshooting

Ethernet Networks

Byron Spinney

pb

**PROFESSIONAL
PRESS BOOKS**

Copyright © 1992 Professional Press Books

All rights reserved. No part of this publication may be reproduced, stored in a retrieval system, or transmitted in any form or by any means whatsoever, except in the case of brief quotations embodied in critical reviews and articles.

The information in this book is subject to change without notice and should not be construed as a commitment by the author or the publisher. Although every precaution has been taken in the preparation of this book, the publisher assumes no responsibility for errors or omissions.

Printed in the United States of America.

Cover design by Sue Ann Rainey.

Trademark Acknowledgments

DECnet and VMS are registered trademarks of Digital Equipment Corporation.
Ethernet is a trademark of Xerox Corporation.
UNIX is a registered trademark of UNIX System Laboratories, Inc.
All other trademarks are the property of their respective owners.

Library of Congress Cataloging-in-Publication Data

Spinney, Byron, 1960 -
    Ethernet pocket guide : a practical guide to designing,
  installing, and troubleshooting Ethernet networks / Byron Spinney.
        p. cm.
    Includes index.
    ISBN 1-878956-25-6
    1. Ethernet (Local area network system)   I. Title.
  TK51405.8E83S65 1992
  004.6'8--dc20   92-14946
                                                              CIP

Please address comments and questions to the publisher:

Professional Press Books
101 Witmer Road
Horsham, PA 19044
(215) 957-4287 FAX (215) 957-1050
Internet: books@propress.com

Contents

PREFACE

When I started working with computer systems, more than 14 years ago, memory was core and 32 KB was considered a luxury. Networks were in the formative stages. Documentation was scarce, and what could be found was usually written by an engineer for readers with technical backgrounds.

A few years have passed; memory is now semiconductors, and 32 MB is not considered unusual. Networks can be found in practically every company with a few PCs, but good books on getting started are still hard to find. There are many books from which to choose, but few deliver the information that is really needed.

This book was written for anyone who will help with or take charge of the design, installation, or troubleshooting of a simple Ethernet network. It contains information to help you really get started. Basic information is provided about the technical aspects of Ethernet, Ethernet standards, cable types and rules, and hardware and rules. A case study illustrates the theories presented and shows how to put them into practice.

This book is not the answer to all Ethernet questions; it does not address complex networks, nor is it a tutorial on the technical aspects of Ethernet. But if you are interested in getting started with Ethernet networking and you want to learn how to design, install, and troubleshoot basic Ethernet networks, this book is for you.

Good luck.

Chapter **1**

INTRODUCTION

Many different types of networks connect computer systems. The most common types include RS-232, X.25, Ethernet, and Token Ring. Each type comes with its own advantages and liabilities. Some provide high-speed transmission with a relatively high cost per connection; others provide low-cost connections with slower transmission speeds.

WHAT IS ETHERNET?

Ethernet is a networking type designed primarily by Xerox Corporation. Three companies were involved in the development of Ethernet V2.0: Digital Equipment Corporation, Intel Corporation, and Xerox.

Ethernet is made up of a physical layer and a software layer. The physical layer consists of the cabling, transceivers and controllers. The software layer is responsible for transmitting and receiving data and recovering from errors. These layers conform to standards of the Open Systems Interconnect (OSI) model developed by the International Standards Organization (ISO).

THE ISO AND OSI

Most discussions of Ethernet include a reference to the ISO OSI model. The ISO developed a networking model called Open Systems Interconnect to create a common, open method of connecting computer systems to pass information. The OSI is not a network, nor is it a piece of Ethernet. Ethernet adheres to the standards set in layers 1 and 2 of the OSI model, which consists of seven layers (layer 1 is the lowest and layer 7 the highest):

• Layer 1, the physical layer — The physical layer provides the mechanical and electrical connection and the control function. The elements in this layer include the medium (i.e., cabling), transceivers, and Ethernet controllers.

• Layer 2, the data link layer — The data link layer comprises the software that establishes connections, transmits and receives data, detects errors, and releases connections.

• Layer 3, the network layer — The network layer resolves network addresses and provides service selection. This is the layer where the Internet Protocol (IP) of TCP/IP is found.

• Layer 4, the transport layer — Data transmission is controlled at the transport layer. This is the home of the Transmission Control Protocol (TCP) of TCP/IP.

• Layer 5, the session layer — The session layer establishes tables of source and destination addresses so that sessions on different computers on the network can communicate.

• Layer 6, the presentation layer — This layer transfers information from applications to the operating system.

- Layer 7, the application layer — The application layer provides security, electronic mail, and print services, and is where application programs reside.

Ethernet uses the first two layers. However, IP, which operates at layer 3, and TCP, contained in layer 4, constitute the TCP/IP suite of communications protocols. They are found with most UNIX-based systems that use Ethernet and are supported by other operating systems that use Ethernet. It is important to note that TCP/IP is not part of Ethernet.

WHY ETHERNET?

The three major benefits of Ethernet are its flexibility, large installed base, and low cost per connection. Ethernet can be implemented across multiple platforms and easily expanded. Almost every major computer vendor provides an Ethernet connection to its system, as a standard element or as an option. PC systems require network interface cards, but these cards are generally inexpensive. And it is easy to find tools to perform file and data transfer when Ethernet connects dissimilar systems.

WHY NOT ETHERNET?

A disadvantage of Ethernet is that there are not enough testing tools to debug and predict traffic overloading on Ethernet networks. Recently, many vendors have introduced management and diagnostic software, though.

In addition, Ethernet has a transmission speed of 10 Mbps. Although this is an excellent rate, higher than many others, some networks are much faster and more efficient than Ethernet.

There are also problems related to traffic loading with Ethernet. This issue has been a topic of wide debate and is addressed later in this chapter.

HOW ETHERNET TRANSMITS

Ethernet uses packets to transmit data. Each packet contains information about the sender, the intended receiver, the type or length of packet, actual data, and a cyclic redundancy check (CRC). See "The Ethernet Packet" section later in this chapter for more information on packets.

When a node is ready to send a packet, it listens to the network for traffic. If the node does not detect any traffic, it proceeds to transmit. This process is called *carrier sense*. The signals that carry network traffic and information are called *carriers*.

Because no other contention or permission mechanism allows or forbids a node to transmit, the network is said to permit *multiple access*. Even though packets are transmitted at approximately 70 percent the speed of light, two or more nodes may transmit at the same time. An example of a network type that uses a contention method is Token Ring, which allows a node to transmit only when it possesses the token.

When two nodes transmit simultaneously, a collision occurs. Network hardware can detect collisions. The term for this process is *collision detection*. When a collision occurs, each of the transmitting nodes continues to transmit for a brief period, propagating the collision throughout the network to make it aware of the collision. After the transmission of the jam signal is complete, each of the transmitting nodes waits a random period of time and then attempts to retransmit its packets.

If a node retransmitting a message because of a collision detects that the message has been involved in another collision, the controller varies the waiting period before the next transmission. Instead of waiting a random period of time, the node waits twice the previous time and then retransmits the message. If the message is involved in another collision, this process is repeated, twice the last waiting time for each occurrence, until the message has been involved with a predetermined number of collisions, usually 16. When the maximum number of collisions has occurred, the controller ceases attempting to transmit and generates an error message. This method of transmission is called Carrier Sense Multiple Access with Collision Detection (CSMA/CD).

ETHERNET EFFICIENCY

Because Ethernet is a statistically based topology, the issue of network loading and saturation is cloudy. Ethernet networks can be tuned in several different ways; tuning factors include protocols used, buffering, and communications characteristics.

Protocols

There are many protocols for transmitting information over Ethernet. Some are extremely efficient;

others are not. The deficient protocols provide little logic to ensure that the data fields of the Ethernet packets are full, and the efficient protocols use logic to ensure that every packet that can carry a full data field does so. The efficient protocols transfer more data with fewer packets. The fewer packets transmitted, the lower the chance of a collision. Thus, more data is transferred in a shorter period of time.

Buffering

Buffering is another factor in Ethernet's efficiency. Buffering allows a controller to make the most efficient use of its time on the wire by allowing packets to be collected in the buffer before transmission. When the packets are all collected in the buffer, the controller waits for a period of quiet and then is able to transmit for the full amount of time allotted. If the controller can begin its transmission collision free, it can send the maximum number of packets in the allowed time. This method greatly reduces the statistical chance of a collision, since a collision can occur only at the beginning of a transmission.

Communications Characteristics

Communications characteristics describe how the network is used; that is, how many users access it, how frequently, and how they make use of it. If one user sends data to a receiver, the user should be able to get the full bandwidth from the cable, or close to 100 percent efficiency. The more users who transmit, and the increased frequency of their transmissions, the higher the probability of collisions and the lower the efficiency.

THE ETHERNET PACKET

The basic Ethernet packet, or frame, contains 6 bytes
for the destination, 6 bytes for the source, 2 bytes for
the type or length of field, 46 to 1,500 bytes for the
data field, and 4 bytes for the frame check sequence.
(See Figure 1-1.) The destination address contains the
Ethernet address of the intended destination, and the
source address contains the address of the transmitting source. The type/length field indicates the type of
packet (Ethernet V2) or the length of the data being
transmitted (802.3-compliant Ethernet). The data
area contains the data being sent, such as data from a
file that is being sent from one system to another. The
data field minimum is 46 bytes, even if only 1 byte is
being sent. If the file being transmitted is larger than
1,500 bytes, multiple packets are sent. The frame
check sequence is a mathematically produced figure
that represents the checksum value of the packet and
is used to detect transmission errors.

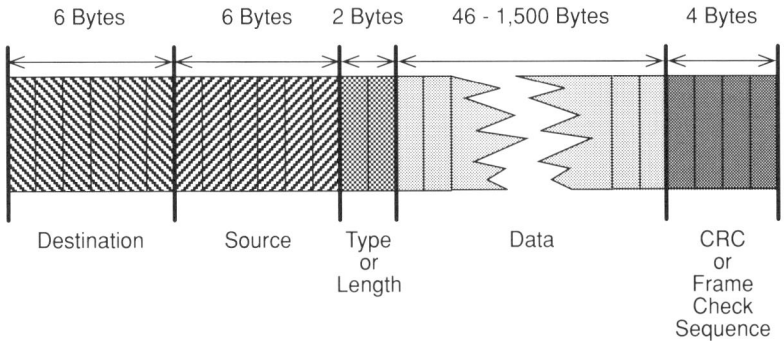

6 Bytes	6 Bytes	2 Bytes	46 - 1,500 Bytes	4 Bytes
Destination	Source	Type or Length	Data	CRC or Frame Check Sequence

Figure 1-1. Ethernet Packet

ETHERNET VERSIONS

There are three standards of Ethernet: Ethernet V1, Ethernet V2, and the Institute of Electrical and Electronics Engineers (IEEE) 802.3 standard.

Ethernet V1

Two facts are important to know about Ethernet V1. First, if you are designing a new Ethernet network, you do not need to worry about Ethernet V1. Second, because Ethernet V1 is not compatible with any other Ethernet standard, it is unlikely that you will run across it.

In version 1, data was encoded differently than in version 2. Version 1 detected collisions during packet reception, whereas version 2 and 802.3-compliant Ethernet detect collisions during packet transmission. Version 1 was replaced by version 2 before the IEEE issued the IEEE 802.3 standard.

Ethernet V2

Ethernet V2 installations are very common, but they are not usually installed now. Many new installations are 802.3 compliant.

Ethernet V2 is incompatible with version 1 and, to some minor extent, with the IEEE 802.3 specification. The incompatibility with the 802.3 standard has to do with the type/length field introduced earlier. Ethernet V2 uses this field as a type identifier, and the 802.3 standard uses this field as a length identifier. The difference in how this field is used is most significant

for protocol analyzers that use the version 2 type field
to identify what packet type is being transmitted.

IEEE 802.3

Note that the IEEE 802.3 standard is not Ethernet. It
is a network standard developed by the IEEE. It was,
however, greatly influenced by the Ethernet V2 specification, and Ethernet can conform to it.

Chapter **2**

MEDIA

Many types of media can run Ethernet. Each has its own benefits and liabilities.

The most common types of cable are attachment unit interface (AUI), thick coaxial, thin coaxial, unshielded twisted-pair (UTP), and fiber-optic cable. Thick coaxial and fiber-optic cable are used for baseband and broadband applications. Baseband applications use a single channel. Broadband applications employ many channels; each channel can be used as a separate network segment.

AUI CABLE

AUI cable, commonly called drop cable, is probably the most widely used cable. It most often attaches devices such as workstations to transceivers.

The eight twisted pairs of wires contained in the AUI cable tend to make it a little stiff and cumbersome to work with. This cable terminates at either end with connectors called *D plugs*, each of which has 15 pins. The male end of the cable typically connects to the equipment, and the female end usually connects to the transceiver. (See Figure 2-1.)

AUI Cable
Assembly

Female Connector

Slide-Latch Assembly

Male Connector

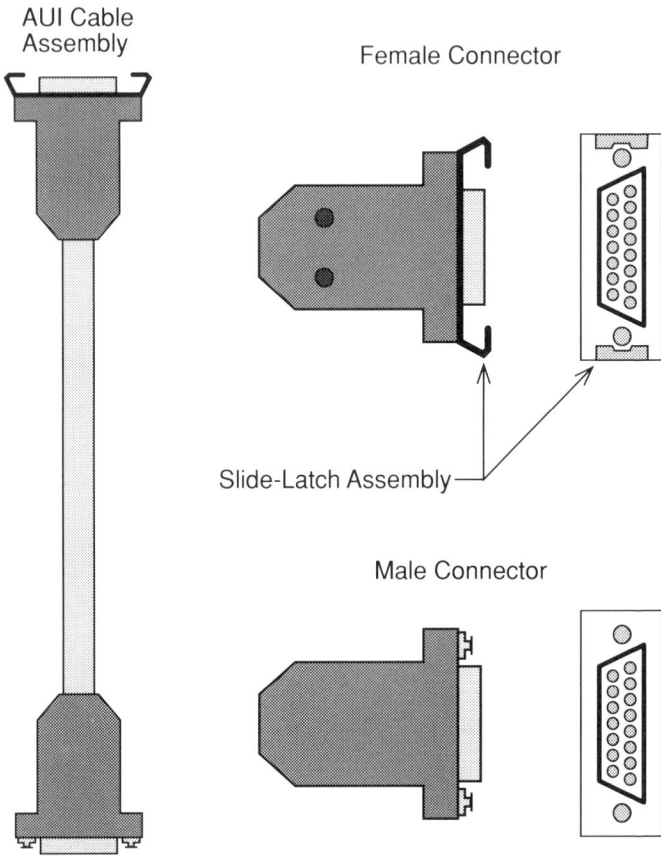

Figure 2-1. AUI Cable and Connectors

On the female connector is a slide-latch assembly
used to secure the connector to the transceiver. The
same slide-latch assembly is also on the equipment
connector. These assemblies are marginal at best.
They are made from a soft metal and bend very easily, providing an excellent source of network headaches. Take your time when making these connections, and make sure that the cables do not pull on
the connectors.

The maximum cable length for AUI cable is 50 meters,
or 164.5 feet. (See Figure 2-2.)

THICK COAXIAL CABLE

Thick coaxial cable (the cable type specified by the
IEEE 10Base-5 standard) is most often used as a network backbone. The network backbone is what it
sounds like — the spine to which the network connects. All network hardware is interconnected
through the common backbone cable. (See Figure 2-3.)

The thick coaxial cable consists of a single copper center conductor covered with a dielectric material,
which in turn is covered by a braid of copper wire, all
of which is contained in a polyvinyl chloride or teflon-
type jacket. The teflon jacket is used in applications
requiring fire-resistant cabling. Because coaxial cable
is thick, it can be a little difficult to work with. The
cable is marked with a stripe every 2.5 meters for tap
attachment. It is terminated at either end by N-type
connectors. At each of the cable's terminating ends, a
50-ohm terminator is required.

Benefits	Liabilities

AUI Cable

Standard cable for workstation connection.	Slide-latch assembly provides poor connection reliability.
	Restrictive length rule.

Thick Coaxial Cable

Maximum length of 500 meters.	Taps can be troublesome.
Cable is marked every 2.5 meters for tap attachment.	Somewhat difficult handling.

Plastic Fiber-Optic Cable

Excellent immunity from EMI and RFI.	Can be run for significantly shorter distances than glass fiber-optic cable.
Significantly easier installation of connectors than glass fiber-optic cable.	Expensive test equipment.

Glass Fiber-Optic Cable

Impervious to EMI and RMI.	High termination costs.
Offers extended length.	More labor intensive to handle than other media.
	Cable and tools are expensive.

Thin Coaxial Cable

Relatively inexpensive.	Can be run only 185 meters.
Easy to terminate.	Lower resistance to noise insertion than thick coaxial or
Easy to handle.	fiber-optic cable.

Twisted-Pair Cable

Less expensive than other media.	Can be run only 100 meters.
Easier to handle and terminate than other media.	

Figure 2-2. Cable Benefits and Liabilities

To get from the baseband coaxial cable to a node, you must install a device called a *noninvasive tap* or sever the cable and install an *inline*, or *invasive*, tap. These taps should be installed only on the stripes provided on the cable jacket. A transceiver is attached to the tap, and an AUI cable is attached to the transceiver to connect the node.

The maximum length for thick coaxial cable is 500 meters, or 1,640 feet. The maximum number of transceivers per segment is 100. The minimum transceiver separation is 2.5 meters. The transceivers should be spaced on a multiple of 2.5 meters (e.g., 2.5, 5, 7.5, 10). (See Figure 2-2.)

FIBER-OPTIC CABLE

Fiber-optic cable provides an excellent broadband backbone. There are two types of fiber-optic cables, plastic and glass. Both contain fiber strands sheathed by an insulating material.

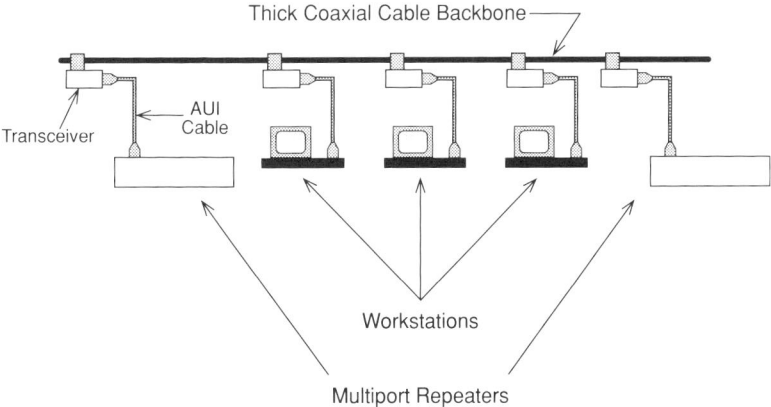

Figure 2-3. Network Backbone

Plastic Fiber

Although plastic fiber is more resilient and easier to handle than glass fiber (it is fairly easy to terminate with a connector), it does have some handling restrictions. The disadvantages of plastic fiber-optic cabling include high attenuation and low bandwidth, which translate into significantly shorter distance specifications and lower data rates than glass fiber cables entail.

The number of fiber strands and the size of the strands in a cable are based on your application. (See Figure 2-2.)

Glass Fiber

Glass fiber cable has some significant restrictions. It must be handled with care and installed carefully. The number and size of the fibers are application specific.

The most notable liability of glass fiber is the cost to terminate. A fiber specialist must polish and inspect each strand of fiber before the connector can be attached. This process requires a lot of time and money.

Another liability of glass fiber is that it degrades over time. Heat and cold cause glass fibers to expand and contract until they fracture. The optics also become discolored by heat and cold and particle radiation. This discoloration causes a gradual decrease in bandwidth.

The most noteworthy benefits of glass fiber are its minimal distance restrictions and imperviousness to electromagnetic interference (EMI) and radio frequency interference (RFI). (See Figure 2-2.)

THIN COAXIAL CABLE

Thin coaxial cable (the cable type specified by the IEEE 10Base-2 standard) applications are commonly called *thinnet* or *cheapernet*. They use a 50-ohm co-axial cable that is flexible and easy to handle. These cables are terminated with BNC connectors that are easy to connect.

The major liability of thin coaxial cable is its length limitation. Its maximum segment length is 185 meters. It also allows only 30 transceiver connections per segment.

It is recommended to use a coaxial cable with a stranded center conductor. This conductor is more resilient as the cable is flexed. (See Figure 2-2.)

TWISTED-PAIR CABLE

The use of twisted-pair cable for 10-Mbps transmission (the cable type specified by the IEEE 10Base-T standard) is becoming very popular. According to the IEEE 802.3i-1990 specification, the design objective for running twisted-pair cable was 100 meters. However, longer lengths are permitted, provided that they meet the requirements of section 14.4 of the IEEE standard. Because the performance parameters and the 100-meter goal are generally met with a 0.5mm-diameter, 24-guage, telephone twisted-pair cable, the maximum distance supported depends on the cable specifications and the manufacturer selected.

Twisted pair is the least expensive medium to install. Its price per foot and cost to install is typically less than the other media. Even the connectors cost less. Often, existing phone cabling can be used for wiring.

Take caution, though, when considering twisted-pair cable. The maximum cable length is determined by the cable's specifications and the manufacturer of the supporting equipment. Do not lock yourself into a piece of hardware by running your cable over 150 meters because the equipment allows you to. You may wish to replace that equipment some day.

The biggest advantage to twisted pair is that many buildings have 24-guage telephone cabling already in place that could be used for a network. This benefit greatly reduces the cost of the installation. (See Figure 2-2.)

Chapter 3

NETWORK HARDWARE

Five main hardware components are used in Ethernet networks: transceivers, repeaters and multiport repeaters, bridges, routers, and gateways. However, not every Ethernet network has all five; many have only one or two.

In general, you should purchase hardware that provides some informative display, such as light-emitting diodes (LEDs), so that you can quickly ascertain how the hardware is functioning.

TRANSCEIVERS

The transceiver is the most common hardware element in an Ethernet network. Usually packaged in a 1- x 4- x 4-inch box, the transceiver allows an AUI cable to connect to another medium, such as thick coaxial cable. The transceiver provides the mechanism to transfer the signal from the coaxial cable to the AUI cable and vice versa. The transceiver can also generate the signal quality error (SQE) signal.

Transceivers are most commonly used to run drop cables from a thick coaxial spine to individual systems. However, some transceivers convert to an AUI cable from thin coaxial, twisted pair, and fiber. (See Figure 3-1.)

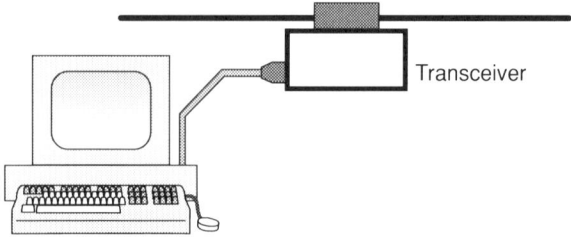

Transceiver

Transceiver Detail

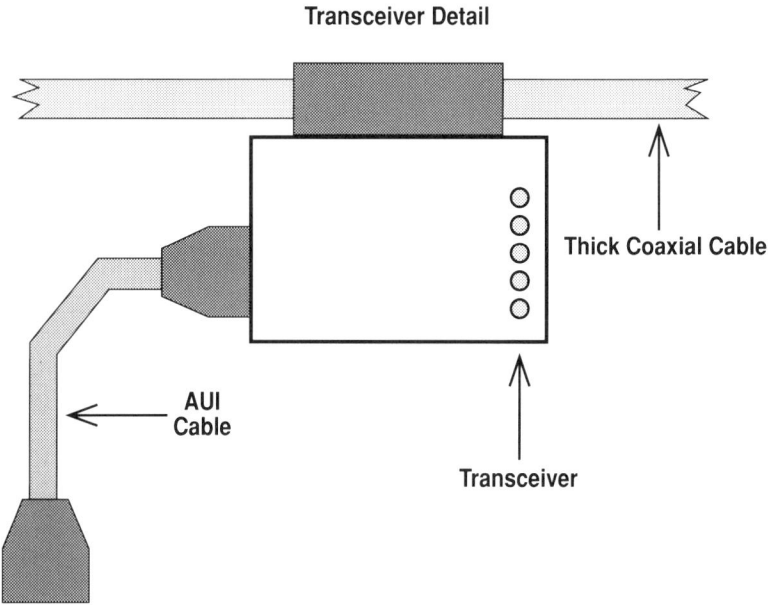

Thick Coaxial Cable

AUI Cable

Transceiver

Figure 3-1.   Transceiver Application

REPEATERS AND MULTIPORT REPEATERS

The function of a repeater is very straightforward — to repeat an incoming signal. The basic repeater connects two segments of Ethernet within the same local area network (LAN). The repeater receives a signal from either segment and then retransmits it to both segments. The repeater also performs collision checking.

Effectively, repeaters allow the extension of segments beyond the limitations of their length rules. For example, assume you need to run a segment of thick coaxial cable 1,750 meters, but the cable can run only a maximum of 1,500 meters. If a repeater were installed 900 meters from one end of the segment, no length rule would be violated. The 900-meter and 850-meter sections would be considered separate segments, each having a 1,500-meter limit. (See Figure 3-2.)

Rules restricting the number of repeaters between nodes vary among manufacturers. Some say two; many more say four. The number must be restricted

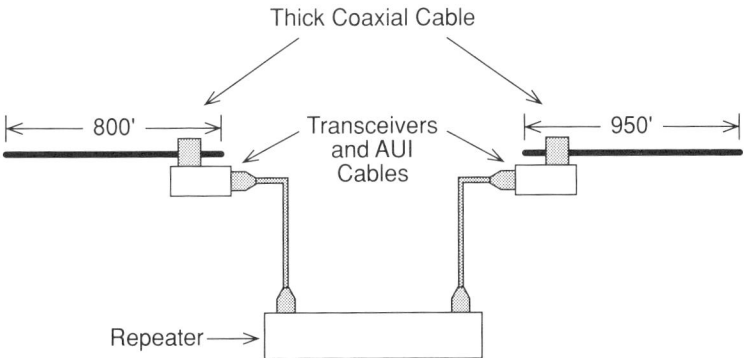

Figure 3-2. Repeater Between Two Thick Coaxial Segments

because repeaters introduce timing problems when they receive and retransmit signals.

Multiport repeaters connect more than two segments. Their major application is connecting to the thick co-axial backbone and servicing an area that uses different cabling, such as thin coaxial, AUI, or twisted pair. (See Figure 3-3.)

Another common application of multiport repeaters is the use of all thin coaxial cable, without a thick coaxial backbone. In this case, two or more multiport repeaters are interconnected by a segment of thin coaxial cable so that they repeat on thin coaxial cable as well. This is a very common application for small-to-medium-sized installations.

Multiport repeaters are also used alone. In an application of less than 20 segments, a multiport repeater can provide all the service. In this case, there is no backbone cable; each segment simply runs to the multiport repeater. (See Figure 3-3.)

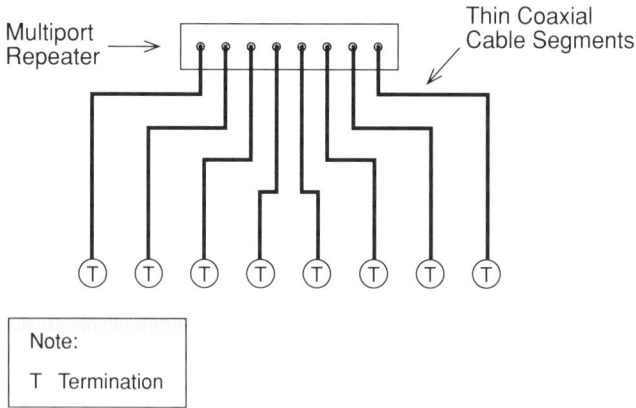

Figure 3-3. Multiport Repeater

BRIDGES

Bridges resemble repeaters in that they join two segments of a network. However, a repeater sees all packets on both or all segments, whereas a bridge passes
only those packets destined for a node on the other
side. As with a repeater, the segments on either side of
the bridge are considered separate in terms of length
rules. Thus, a designer can use bridges both to extend
the length of a segment and to isolate traffic. Bridges
are most often used to segregate busy networks.

Bridges connect LAN segments using the same physical-layer protocol; for example, an Ethernet segment
to another Ethernet segment. To connect segments
using dissimilar physical-layer protocols, such as
Ethernet and Token Ring, you would use a gateway.
Gateways are discussed further in this chapter.

If a network is sluggish because it is overloaded with
traffic, a bridge may be the answer. If a group of
nodes produces heavy traffic and those nodes are communicating mostly among themselves, it may be best
to install a bridge to separate this group from the
other nodes. The users in the low-usage group will
experience an increase in network throughput. The
other group will also experience an increase in network throughput, but, depending on the amount of
traffic it is producing, this group may not notice the
increased performance as often as the lower usage
group does. (See Figure 3-4.)

Clearly, the network designer or administrator must
understand the characteristics of the network to place

the bridge at the point that will provide the maximum benefit.

The bridge can help only with traffic on the network. Performance problems caused by a server that cannot handle the processing load or applications that are poorly written for network use cannot be solved with a bridge.

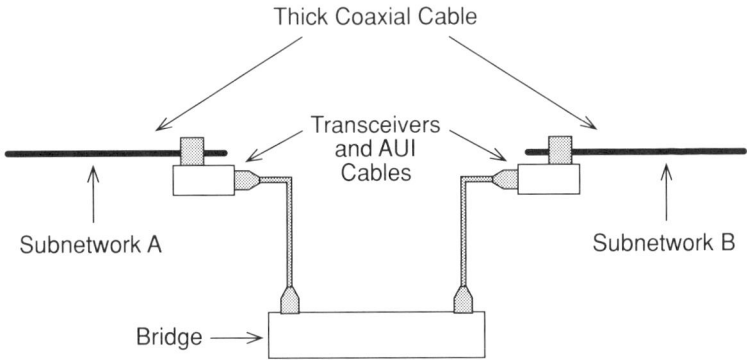

Figure 3-4. Bridge Connecting Two Thick Coaxial Segments

ROUTERS

A router performs the same functions as a bridge. Plus, for more money than a bridge, a router filters.

The concept of filtering is relatively simple. A router is programmed with a set of rules that tell it what type of packets may pass in which direction on the network. Consider the following example. A network administrator who wants only TCP Simple Mail Transfer Protocol (SMTP) traffic to cross from subnetwork A to subnetwork B can program the router to filter out all other types of packets.

The programming of routers varies by manufacturer. But it is not very difficult once you understand the basic concepts. (See Figure 3-5.)

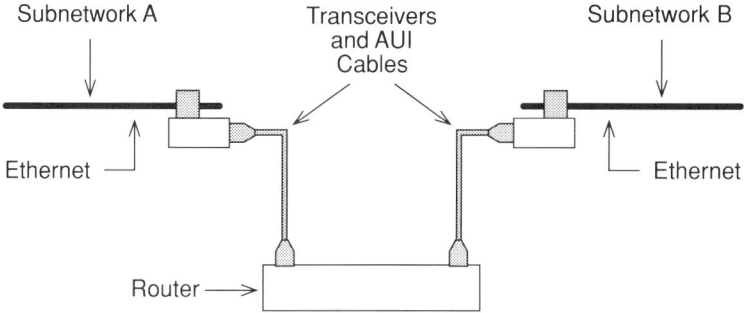

Figure 3-5. Router Connecting Two Ethernet Networks

GATEWAYS

A gateway is like a bridge in that it passes only packets bound for the other side. More expensive than the bridge, a gateway connects dissimilar network types. For example, a gateway could connect an Ethernet network and a Token Ring network. The gateway translates from one protocol to the other and handles differences in data format, speed, and signal levels. (See Figure 3-6.)

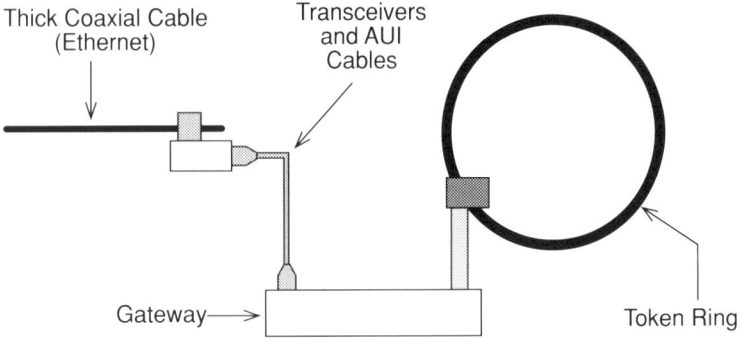

Figure 3-6. Gateway Connecting an Ethernet and Token Ring Network

Chapter 4

NETWORK DESIGN

The network designer is in a very precarious position. On one side are the expectations of users and management, and on the other side are the hard realities of design restrictions, time requirements, and budgetary needs. Designers must discern a network's real needs and objectives and communicate them. To do this, they must be bold, brave, meticulous, and innovative.

The bold designer communicates effectively to management, creating realistic expectations. The brave designer stands up to vendors, unmoved by what everyone else is doing. The meticulous designer checks and double-checks a design against the rules and documents everything. The innovative designer sees obstacles as opportunities, finding simple solutions in impossible situations. All four types of designers consider both the short- and long-term ramifications of their designs.

THREE BASIC RULES

While working through a design, a designer should follow these three rules to keep out of serious trouble:

- Keep it simple.

- Document everything.

- Stay within the rules.

Keep It Simple

Complexity leads to nightmares. Simple designs are manageable and maintainable. Design simplicity includes:

- Keeping the changes in media to a minimum.

- Allowing easy access to all hardware and cables.

- Minimizing the number of nodes per leg.

To design simply, you must consider the needs of the management and maintenance of the network.

Media Changes. It is usually best to design a network with only one type of medium, since one type is generally easier and less expensive to manage and maintain. However, it is not always possible or wise to use only one type. You must evaluate your network requirements.

A single medium type is easier and less expensive to manage and maintain because every medium has different installation, maintenance, and test equipment requirements. Also, when different media types are connected, hardware connections and special equipment are necessary. Each of these connections and pieces of equipment can create additional problems.

Hardware and Media Access. When designing a network, you must consider how it will be maintained. At some installations, maintenance personnel must damage walls to get to existing cable, or they need a 30-foot ladder to reach the transceivers in the rafters. If you imagine that you are going to service and expand your network, you will avoid many problems for the people who do. For example, you should install a conduit for network cable in walls; this conduit allows additions and deletions of cable with minimal effort.

Minimize the Number of Nodes. When designing a network with a topology that allows more than a single node per leg, such as thinnet, try to minimize the number of nodes per leg. The reason is very simple. If there is a problem on a leg with 20 nodes (e.g., the failure of the port on the multiport repeater), then 20 nodes are affected by the problem. However, if there are only 10 nodes on that leg, only 10 nodes are affected.

Document Everything

There was an excellent electrical engineer who, when asked to explain his design prowess, advised others to "Write it all down." When asked, "Who has time to write it down?" he responded, "Someone who does not have time to relearn." How does documenting failures and successes, thoughts and ideas, help make you a good designer? The further you progress in the design and implementation of a project, the more important documentation becomes.

A design journal explains the logic, long forgotten, of why one solution was selected over another. It creates a comprehensive history of "what happened when...." A journal can come to the rescue when management asks why some part of the design is done a certain way, helping you explain how the implementation methodology was chosen.

During the installation phase, a design journal provides answers to difficult problems that often appear. For example, when an unforeseen obstacle blocks the path of a leg, the journal can say whether other repeaters have ports to draw from and whether these repeaters will provide the same connectivity as the original path. Time saved in making such decisions helps to keep the installation on time and in budget.

During maintenance, the journal will provide a history showing why the network is in its present configuration and suggest how to expand or change the network's topology. For example, a department with both a companywide and a private LAN running into its offices might decide to allow another department to connect to its private LAN. The design journal would detail how the LANs are separated and might offer some options for connecting the LANs without providing access to the private LAN elsewhere in the company.

The design journal should be a permanent-bound notebook with graph paper and prenumbered pages. The permanent binding prevents the unnoticed loss of pages. The graph paper provides ruled lines to write on and graphs for drawing diagrams. The prenumbered pages facilitate your referencing previously recorded thoughts or events.

Stay Within the Rules

Beware of vendors who tell you, "It's OK, I've seen lots of sites with lines that long." *Never* invite disaster by compromising your design. A good design identifies its own boundaries and works within them by a comfortable margin.

Some manufacturers design their equipment to perform beyond normal Ethernet specifications; some say they will allow you to run lines beyond the distances recommended. If your design requires extra capability, you must decide whether to take the manufacturer's offer or find another solution to the problem. To help make this decision, find out if any other major manufacturers offer the same capabilities. If they do, ask whether their equipment is compatible with your selected manufacturer's. Next, investigate the costs of working around the restriction that is causing you to consider breaking design rules. You should not design a network that is manufacturer specific. If your relationship with the manufacturer becomes strained or the manufacturer goes out of business and its products and support are no longer available, you will want the ability to switch manufacturers without replacing hardware or redesigning parts of the network.

RULES

The following rules for leg length, node numbers, and hardware usage will help to keep your design stable.

Lengths

As you will remember from Chapter 2, each type of medium has a length restriction. It is best to never exceed 80 percent of the allotted length for any leg or segment. It is often best to spend a little extra on hardware—for example, for extra ports on a multiport repeater—to avoid having a leg that is almost too long.

Number of Nodes

The total number of nodes allowable on a network segment is 1,024. A segment is considered a complete network comprising one or more legs that can stand alone. Segments can be connected through repeaters or bridges to extend the length or capacity of the network.

You should also consider how many nodes are allowed per leg. A leg is any length of medium that connects one or more nodes to a network. The number of nodes per leg should be ten or less so that if there is a failure in the physical layer of one of the legs, the number of nodes affected will be minimal.

Hardware

The most notable hardware rule is that no more than two repeaters may be placed between two nodes. Some manufacturers claim that they will support more. If you choose to install more than two repeaters between two nodes, learn as much as possible about the capabilities of different manufacturers. You want to avoid becoming locked into a single manufacturer.

DESIGN STEP ONE

Step one in the design process is to identify the network's usage characteristics. To do this, you must understand the needs, goals, and desires of each group that will use the network. Asking the following questions can help you gain this knowledge:

- Who in each group will use the network?

- How will each person use the network?

  — For file transfers?

  — For printing?

  — For data storage or retrieval?

  — For communications (electronic mail)?

  — For terminal servers?

  — For file or application sharing?

- How often will each person use the network?

- How long will that person use the network?

- What will be the daily, weekly, and monthly peak times for usage?

- Who will need to communicate with whom, and how?

When these questions are answered, you can start to ask the next set of questions:

- How large are the files that will be transferred, and how often will they be sent?

- How large are the files that will be printed, and how often will they be printed?

- How large are the files that will be printed on a PostScript printer, and how often will this occur?

- How often will files be stored on and retrieved from servers, and how large will they be?

- Will network electronic mail involve many file attachments? What size will the attached files be? How often will they be transmitted?

- If terminal servers will be put on the network, how much traffic will they generate? Traffic generation is a function of the server protocol and the usage level of the server. Some protocols, such as local area transport (LAT), are very efficient, whereas some are not. No matter how efficient a protocol is, you still need to consider the server's usage level.

- If files, applications, or databases will be shared across a network, how much activity will this sharing entail, based on the size of the files or data structures and the estimated frequency of transmittal?

Lastly, you will need to know the following:

- Are any areas that the network will serve affected by environmental concerns (e.g., weather, EMI, or physical stress)?

- What geographical concerns must be considered? Will the network run between separate floors or buildings?

Answering these questions can help you quantify the usage and needs of your network by group and physical area. It will enable you to make decisions about segmentation, required hardware, and media types.

DESIGN STEP TWO

Step two is one of the hardest. First, you must try to make sense of the traffic information you collected during the previous step. This can be very trying because the information gathered does not provide hard, quantifiable numbers that you can place in simple formulas to tell you what is going on.

Without expensive equipment and specialized test environments, the best you can do is to get a feel for how the network will work with different types of traffic. You must infer this from historical data gathered from an existing network's performance. If you currently have a network, try to identify usage patterns that match those in your survey. If you do not have a network, ask some other network managers about patterns on their networks that match those on your survey. Or ask the vendor of your networking products what other customers with usages like yours have experienced. However, putting blind trust in another network manager's advice can prove foolish. The same is true with vendors. A little misinformation, intentional or not, can put you in a very bad spot.

If you are fortunate enough to have a network to survey, ask the following questions:

- How do the patterns that you can identify affect network usage?

- Can you identify any types of network processes that cause a degradation of speed?

From your information, extrapolate performance parameters and the issues you will encounter with the new network. You must also identify the nodes with a sufficiently high traffic level to slow the network.

With a sense of what type of traffic problems you might encounter and where, and how they might arise, you can decide where to install bridges and routers to isolate segments and reduce the traffic on each segment.

If you have no network from which to gather historical data, or do not feel much confidence in your information sources, you should consider hiring a consultant with experience in network design. A consultant can help quantify your network load and identify where, if at all, you should install bridges or routers. To choose a consultant, interview several and ask them the following questions to learn about their experience and abilities:

- How many networks have you designed that are like mine?

- What are your references? (Local ones are of special interest.)

It may be best to consider consultants who sell only their own expertise and not other products. That way, they will not push inventories on you or feel pressure to sell you a certain product. It is always in your best interest to call references to thoroughly check out the consultant.

DESIGN STEP THREE

Step three is to identify the location of equipment closets, hazards, and nodes. First you must have a copy of the facility's layout marked with the location of each node and all electrical equipment with large transformers or motors, such as industrial machinery. Any other hazards should also be noted.

Next, identify the location of equipment closets where such hardware as multiport repeaters and bridges will be located. If possible, these closets should be centralized to minimize the distances run for each leg.

DESIGN STEP FOUR

Step four is to select the media to construct the network, based on the area in which it will be installed. Consider such factors as noise induction and cable accessibility.

In addition, because fire codes vary from state to state and county to county, make sure that your cable's jacket type is acceptable in your area. For example, most cable comes in a PVC jacket that is acceptable in some parts of California for use in walls, but in other parts of the state, only cables rated as fire resistant are allowed. According to the National Electrical Code, cable with special fire-resistant jackets is required throughout the United States when cable is run in a plenum. (A plenum is an airspace used for air flow. For example, an office that uses the space between the roof and the top of the drop ceiling as a return area for the air conditioning is using it as a plenum.) The main reason for the special cables is to reduce the airborne toxins in a burning building.

Fiber-Optic Cable

You might choose fiber-optic cable for environments with high noise induction. When selecting this cable, use glass if you can afford it. Find a vendor that can talk intelligently about the cable, and remember that your application will decide how many conductors and what diameter of fiber will be best suited for it. A good vendor can also help you select racking accessories for providing the proper radius of bend for the cable as it is terminated in equipment cabinets.

Twisted-Pair Cable

Because a twisted-pair leg supports only a single node, you will need to run a separate cable to each node from the closet. If you are considering using twisted-pair cable, talk to at least two manufacturers. Some manufacturers offer options in this area. Again, be careful not to lock yourself into using any one manufacturer. For twisted-pair cable, the IEEE standard 802.3i-1990 specification states that the normal wiring consists of 0.4- to 0.6-mm diameter, 26- to 22-gauge, unshielded wire in a multipair cable. It is recommended that the minimum cable specification be 0.5-mm, 24-gauge cable, and a .06-mm diameter, 22-gauge cable would be even better.

Thin Coaxial Cable

Thin coaxial cable allows you to use Ethernet as it was originally intended to be used — in a bus topology. The cable can be run from the equipment closet and stitched through several offices before being terminated. Remember that no more than ten nodes should be installed per leg, to minimize impact if the integrity of a leg is compromised.

When selecting thin coaxial cable, choose the medium carefully. Section 7.3.1.1.1 of the Ethernet V2 specification states that the average characteristic impedance of the cable should be 50 ohms, + or - 2 ohms. The most commonly used thin coaxial cable is RG58-AU. And a coaxial cable with a stranded center conductor is better than one with a solid center. The stranded center conductor is much more resilient when flexed.

Thick Coaxial Cable

Baseband coaxial cable is usually available from the manufacturer as *Ethernet cable*. Normally, the cable is yellow or orange and is striped every 2.5 meters. (The color is not important.) The stripe indicates the minimum distance for tap spacing. If you select baseband cable for part of your network, think about how you will access the transceivers and taps when troubleshooting.

DESIGN STEP FIVE

When selecting cable connectors, go first class. This does not necessarily mean buy the most expensive connectors, but it does mean buy the highest quality. Check the quality of connection that the connector makes, the ease of assembly of the connector, and its robustness.

Make sure the connectors are right for the cable you choose. It should fit perfectly, physically and electrically.

When using thin coaxial cable, buy BNC connectors that have a 50-ohm impedance rating.

There are many methods for getting the same result with a connector. For example, BNC connectors for thin coaxial cable have two major methods of connector assembly. With one method, a center pin is soldered in place and then the body is tightened on with a small set of wrenches. This method is referred to as a *can wrench assembly*. But it has proved a bit unreliable. Some people solder better than others; some technicians tighten the assembly too much, causing damage, and some do not tighten the assembly enough, creating an unstable connection.

The other, more popular method is the crimp-style connector. With this method, the center pin is crimped to the center conductor, and a sleeve piece crimps onto the braid. Both of the connections are gas tight if done properly. With crimp-style connectors, good tools aid in making an almost foolproof connection every time.

After selecting the connectors, buy the proper tools. You should buy the tools that are easiest to use, perform best, and are most robust. A high-quality tool helps to ensure a proper termination every time.

Before making a final decision on connectors, get a length of cable and use the selected tools and connectors to make about a dozen connections. Your tools should be efficient, and the connections should be tight but not overly tight. Make sure that the connections look clean, with no braid showing on the coaxial connectors. Also see that the connection process is very effective. For example, crimp tools that ratchet and do not release until the proper crimp has been applied are much more desirable than ones that do not. The crimp tool without the ratchet provides a different amount of crimp each time it is used, providing an inconsistent connection. There is no foolproof tool, but there are many excellent choices.

DESIGN STEP SIX

Next, draw the cable runs on the floor plan. To do this properly you must identify the location of all hardware closets and nodes.

Locate the areas most suitable for installing such devises as multiport repeaters, bridges, and routers. These areas should have adequate ventilation to keep the equipment from overheating and should be readily accessible for servicing. You should not enclose a piece of equipment such as a transceiver in a ceiling or crawl space. Equipment that is not readily accessible will be difficult to troubleshoot and repair. Ensure that clean power is available for these locations.

Measure each run as accurately as possible. Allow a margin of at least 10 percent to cover slack. Visit the site with the drawing and confirm that the route chosen for each run is realistic. You should also review the lengths of each run. Look for such obstacles as beams or soffets that will cause the length of the run to be extended. Try to make sure that each path is accessible after the network is fully operational, although this may not always be possible. Keep in mind that someone will eventually have to service the cable.

Decide where multiple cables can be run at the same time, to reduce installation time and decrease the likelihood of cable burn. This occurs when a cable is pulled across a stationary cable; the resulting friction wears on the outer insulation of the fixed cable, causing many types of problems, the most troublesome being random grounding.

When investigating runs, make sure that there are no threats to the integrity of the cable. For example, do not plan to run cable through the supports for plumbing. (See Figure 4-1.) As the building heats and cools and as the earth shifts, the cable will become pinched between the pipe and its support, and the cable will be severed, or a short will result. Either of these problems will prove difficult to pinpoint. Identify where cable troughs or ladders should be put in. They will help to protect the cable and will provide a permanent supported path for it.

Where the cable comes down from the ceiling, there should be a plastic or metal conduit running from three to six inches above the top plate to the top of the mud ring. (See Figure 4-2.) The conduit provides an efficient way to move or add cable at a location.

Design to keep the cable runs as short and neat as possible. The less often cable has to go around, over, under, or through such obstacles as plumbing and vents, the better.

As you plan your cable route, look for potential sources of RFI and EMI. Electrical lines and fluorescent light are the most common in business environments. Electric motors and heavy appliances are other sources. If you are not using a fiber-optic cable, try to run your cable a minimum of six inches from standard electrical sources. When you must cross an electrical cable or conduit, try to do so at 90 degrees; this will minimize the noise induction to your cable.

As you chart cable routes, you should identify each leg with a unique number sequence — alpha, numeric, or alphanumeric. An identification number should follow the cable all the way back to the repeater, if one is used.

The next step is to identify all of the points of connection. Each point should be designed to avoid random grounding, a problem that usually occurs with thin and thick coaxial cable. This can be avoided by covering the connections with rubber boots.

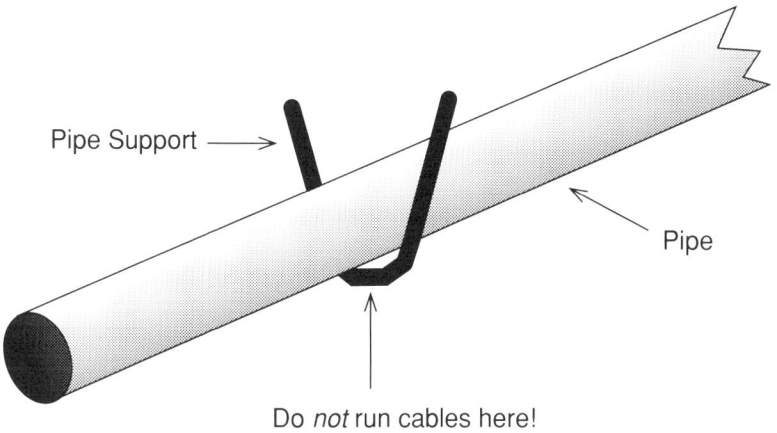

Figure 4-1. Pipe Support

CHOOSING YOUR MANUFACTURER

When selecting hardware, choose the manufacturer with the best track record with your type of application. Look for a manufacturer that is financially stable and offers mature products. You want products with a proven history. This will help to provide a stable networking environment.

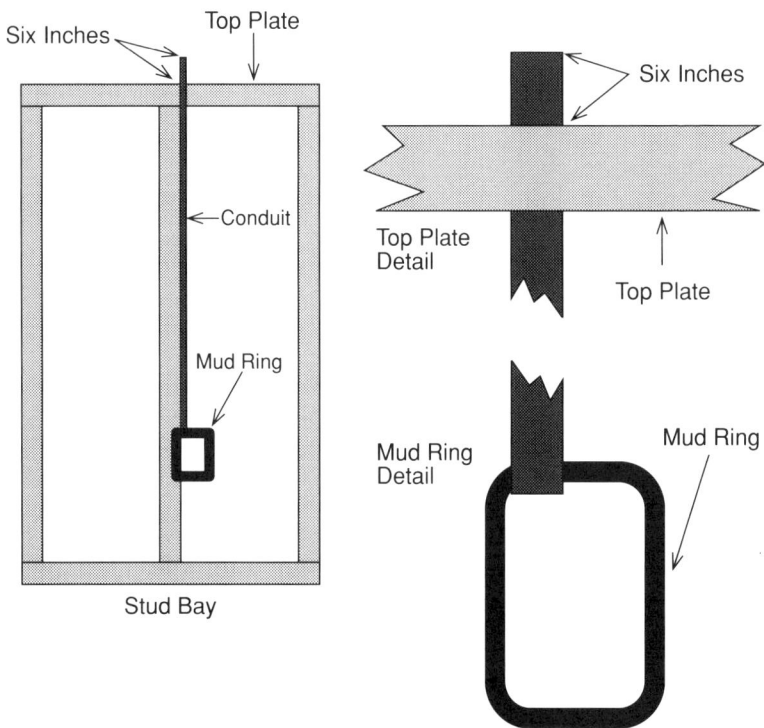

Figure 4-2. Conduit Detail

Many manufacturers now provide equipment with informative lights or displays, which are more than just nice to look at. Some monitor power, heartbeat, collisions, errors, and termination.

SUMMARY

By this point you have:

- Identified the characteristics of the proposed network.

- Quantified the traffic information.

- Identified the location of nodes, hazards, and equipment closets.

- Selected proper media types.

- Selected proper connectors and tools.

- Drawn the cable routes.

- Identified cable trough locations.

- Identified the location of conduits.

- Selected the proper hardware.

The last step in the design process is to double-check everything. Recheck the length of the cable runs, the hardware rules, and hazard locations.

The design process can prove very tedious, with the checking and rechecking and efforts to quantify usage. However, if you are diligent and take the time to give attention to each matter, your design will reward you during installation and troubleshooting.

CASE STUDY

This case study, selected for its simplicity, illustrates each step in network design.

A small investment firm wanted to install a new LAN. The company had 34 employees, 16 of whom used PCs. It had no existing network. At a later date, the company planned to connect a minicomputer to the network. The minicomputer's only networking option was Ethernet 802.3.

The resources to be shared were disks, printers, and a tape drive for network backups. The shared disks would contain spreadsheets, databases, and some accounting information. Through the day, 12 of the 16 employees would access and transfer customer information in the database for use in quote generation. These quotes would be uploaded back into the minicomputer and printed on a PostScript laser printer.

Two of the employees would use the accounting package. Twelve to 14 of the employees would sometimes use a disk to retrieve financial modeling spreadsheets.

The company wanted to add electronic mail at some point. As it was added, each employee would receive a PC.

The network designer had to gather usage information about this network. Having had no previous experience with the kind of usage that this network would entail, the designer turned to the vendor selling the networking hardware, minicomputer, networking software, database program, and quote system. The vendor was also contracting to integrate the modeling spreadsheets onto the network.

The vendor confirmed that the only network interface for the minicomputer was 802.3-compliant Ethernet. It said that several of its clients were using the same packages and computer equipment on networks supporting as many as 40 users. However, it had seen serious performance degradation with busy shops of more than 45 users.

The network designer next examined the facility, noting the location of each PC, the future location of the minicomputer, and possible locations for network hardware.

Next, the designer asked for a set of plans for the facility and scheduled a time to survey the ceiling and space. The ceiling was a drop ceiling with two- by-four-foot tiles. There were two major obstacles. An air conditioning duct cut off the main path to the new computer room, and a fire wall separated four offices from the rest of the building. The air conditioning duct was not on the plans, which the designer had brought to the survey.

The designer measured the length of each run and drew a map of the facility, mapping out a strategy to go around the air conditioning ducts in the main path, even though that path would take much more time to run the cable. The designer also planned where to cut a small hole in the fire wall to pull through the cable. (A small hole would be easy to seal to meet fire codes.)

Because there were no major sources of RFI or EMI in the ceiling or walls, the designer selected thin coaxial cable for the site. The choice was also based on the length of the runs (none greater than 450 feet).

Next, the designer selected a crimp-style BNC connector with a ratcheting crimp tool that would release only when a perfect crimp had been effected. (BNC connectors and tools provide a simple yet highly reliable means of termination.) Also selected was a strip tool that clamped on the end of the cable and that after being spun around the cable three or four times, would cut the isolation at the correct distances from the end in the correct depths.

Next, the designer double-checked the prints for measurements and accuracy.

On the facility plans, the designer indicated where to "stub up" a piece of conduit in the wall to run the coaxial cable down it. The term *stub up* means to install a piece of plastic or metal conduit in a wall from the top of the ring, or access hole, to about six inches above the top plate of the wall.

Knowing that the vendor had reported that as many as 40 people could use the network before degradation would be seen, the designer felt comfortable using a multiport repeater that supported thin coaxial cable. The network would thus contain six legs of thin coaxial cable, all tied to a multiport repeater. The designer also recommended that the company consider using a bridge when the number of network users increased to 35.

This case study is continued at the end of Chapter 5.

Chapter **5**

NETWORK
INSTALLATION

Once the design is done, you must install the network. Although this task can be, and usually is, overwhelming, it does not have to be. Remember the old saying, "The journey of a thousand miles starts with a single step," and resolve to work through the process one task at a time.

Installing a network involves the following efforts:

- Dealing with local officials, such as inspectors and personnel from planning offices.

- Working with contractors.

- Planning work flow.

- Supervising labor.

- Making sure the correct supplies, in the correct quantities, arrive at the correct time.

- Managing scheduling changes.

- Ensuring that cables are run properly and connectors are installed correctly.

- Documenting the whole process.

THE DECISION TO CONTRACT OUT

The first task of installing a network is deciding whether to contract out any of the job, whether to use in-house personnel, or a combination of both. This decision is primarily based on three factors: the scope of the project, the size and qualifications of the available labor pool, and the abilities of the project manager.

Scope of the Project

The scope of each project is driven by three main factors: the size of the project, time constraints, and budget restrictions.

Size of the Project. The size of a project is based on several factors, including the number of node connections being established, the phase that the construction is in when you are scheduled to start work, the type of medium selected, and the physical space involved.

The number of node connections to be established includes every location where a node may some day be attached to the network.

The phase that construction is in when you are scheduled to start is very important. If the construction is not complete, you will want to start your installation before the walls are closed but after all of the framing and most of the mechanical work (including plumbing, electrical work, and HVAC) is completed. If construction is completed, you will have to deal with such issues as how to get cabling into the walls.

The type of medium selected is important because handling and installation techniques are specific to the medium type. Different techniques take different amounts of time. For example, it takes considerably more time to install glass fiber-optic cable than coaxial cable.

The physical space involved in an installation becomes particularly important as multiple floors or buildings are involved.

Time Constraints. Often, the amount of time allotted to install a network is insufficient. Before asking for more time, you should have a clear picture of how long each construction phase will take. You should know:

- How long it will take to get the materials.

- How much time should be allotted to each task.

- How long proper testing will take.

Then, when your questions are answered, draw up a gantt chart of the project.

To get this information, you may need to hire a networking consultant who understands the installation phase. It is important not to underestimate the time necessary to properly install your network.

Budget Restrictions. Rarely is enough money allotted for network installation. Cost projections and what management expects to spend usually differ significantly. Ensure that management understands how much money and time are necessary to accomplish the job.

The Labor Pool

As you are considering whether to hire a consultant, consider the size and qualifications of your labor pool. The installation of a network is not something to be taken lightly. Your network will provide a critical link in the information flow of your department or company.

Managing the Project

Whether the project is kept in house or contracted out, someone from your organization will have to manage it. This person will have to pursue such activities as designing, reviewing designs, researching permit and code requirements, planning for materials, scheduling materials, scheduling labor, verifying that work is being performed to specification, and resolving problems. Be sure to allow enough time for this person to manage the project. If you do not have someone who can properly manage the project, you probably need to hire a professional contractor.

SELECTING A CONTRACTOR

If you decide to subcontract some portion of the project, you will have to select a contractor. Before doing so, clarify just what you want the contractor to do by asking yourself:

- Do you want the contractor to provide all labor and materials?

- Who will be responsible for permits and code restrictions?

- Who will schedule the materials?

- Who will be responsible for communicating requirements to the general contractor?

Once you have a list of exactly what you want the
contractor to do for you and what you are planning to
handle using your company resources, it is time to start
calling contractors.

Where to Look

There are two main sources of contractors. The first and
perhaps most obvious is the phone book. But the second
source — referrals — is better.

To get referrals, call companies in your area that have
networks or seem likely candidates for them and ask
who is in charge of them. Another excellent source is
local user groups. Also, manufacturers often have a list
of contractors in given geographical areas.

How to Interview a Contractor

With your marked blueprints and expectations list at
hand, meet with each proposed contractor in your office.
Explain the scope of the job, which parts you are going
to handle, and which parts a contractor will handle. Be
very specific about the time restrictions, and insist on a
completion time with a margin for error.

Ask each prospective contractor the following questions about his or her company:

- How many years have you been in business?

- Are you licensed with the state?

- Are you bonded?

- Are you insured? For how much?

- How many employees does your company have?

- What are these employees' qualifications?

- Do you have all of the necessary tools to accomplish this job?

Ask each contractor the following questions about his or her work:

- Will you provide a reference list?

- How many jobs of a similar size have you completed?

- How many jobs have you done with my media types?

- Are any of the companies that used these media types on the reference list? If not, will you provide some as references?

- Can you finish the job ahead of schedule? (Doing so would provide some padding.)

- When can you provide a written proposal? (Give a reasonable deadline.)

Making the Final Decision

Your decision on which contractor to select will depend on how each answers your questions and who you feel will work best with you. Almost as important as the chosen contractor's ability is how you two communicate.

If you had trouble in an interview with a contractor's attitude, make a note of it. An attitude that hampers effective communication is very likely to cause trouble as the job progresses. And the more that the contractor interacts with a general contractor on the construction site, the more important communication skills and a positive attitude are. It cannot be overstated that the relationship to the general contractor must never be put in jeopardy because of poor attitudes or communications skills.

After selecting a contractor, you should, as a courtesy, tell all the bidding contractors whether they were chosen.

THE FIRST MEETING

Meet with the contractor and any personnel from your company who are going to help manage the installation. Ensure that each member of this installation planning committee has a copy of both the marked and unmarked blueprints. Review each member's duties and identify any overlapping responsibilities. Stress the importance of communication within the committee. Identify clearly the individuals who can make final decisions in a crunch.

In the first meeting, make sure that each member understands the project's time tables and realizes that it is necessary to clearly document all aspects of the job. Identify dependencies and lay out the first steps toward implementation. Then schedule the next meeting.

As the project continues, meet often with committee members to identify problems and possible solutions.

WHAT TO WATCH FOR

One of the most important tasks in managing an installation is "walking the job." While doing so, keep your eyes open for quality. Do not tolerate activities that detract from the quality of your network. Watch for careless actions, and take your stand against them.

Make sure the documentation is kept consistently. The last thing you want to hear is "Yeah, we'll get to it later." Ensure that notes are legible and drawings are accurate. This documentation will avoid problems someday.

Make sure your media is handled with care. Do not let your crew tug it with force that appears excessive. If that much force is needed, there may be a problem. Take the time to correct it now to save time later.

Watch how connectors are put on. Insist on perfect connections. Although the job of connecting the ends of the cables is very tedious, be sure that no effort is spared to make a perfect connection every time. Bad connections can be one of your worst nightmares; they are hard to find, perform intermittently, and can destroy the confidence of management and users in the stability of a network.

DOCUMENTATION

Documentation should include notes, drawings, measurements, and splice locations. The more detailed your notes, the easier troubleshooting will prove.

Use a stitched lab-style notebook with prenumbered graph pages. Each day place the date at the top of a new page. Keep notes on phone calls, verbal commitments, questions, answers, problems, and solutions in your book. Always note who, what, when, where, and why.

Drawings

In your notebook, keep a copy of every drawing of the facility you are cabling. Each change in its layout usually results in a new drawing; get a copy and keep it. Date all of the drawings and keep them in chronological order.

Make sure that the placement of each cable is detailed in these drawings. Special circumstances or obstacles should be noted. As the installation is completed, make a master print showing all of the cable locations and note all obstacles and special circumstances.

Measurements

As each cable is pulled, record as accurately as possible the amount of cable used for the run. Mark these distances on your drawings. Use counter devices to track the length of cable used as it is pulled off a reel or out of a box. These counters are probably the best bet for accurate measurements.

Splice Locations

Carefully record the location of splices on your drawing. Note the distance from the splice to both ends of the cable. Also indicate the easiest access path to the splice location.

GETTING READY FOR INSTALLATION

Preparing to install the network is a somewhat tedious task, but it will reduce installation and troubleshooting headaches later. The first step is ensuring that your crew members understand their objectives and how to carry out their tasks. See that each member of your team knows whom to contact about problems.

Step two is to make sure that those who are going to put on the connectors have had plenty of practice and are competent. If they are inexperienced, make them practice. The wasted connectors will cost time and money, but you will get a more consistent connection.

Step three is to test the cable in the box or on the spool. The best way to do this is to use a time-domain reflectometer (TDR), which measures cable length and points out any shorts or opens in it. If you do not have a TDR, you can use a volt ohm meter (VOM) to check the continuity of the cable. Fiber-optic cable requires specialized tools.

Testing with a TDR

Inexperienced users cannot usually interpret information provided by a TDR, but in the hands of an experienced user, this testing tool can be extremely helpful for wire media.

A TDR uses a technique much akin to radar. It transmits a signal down the cable and displays the reflection of that signal as a waveform containing information about the cable. This information includes its length; the distance between the TDR and any shorts, opens, or sharp cable bends; and the presence of transceivers, barrel connectors, and terminators.

Before purchasing a TDR, you should strongly consider renting one. Or ask your contractor to provide a TDR, if you are hiring a contractor for some portion of the installation.

Testing with a VOM

You can also use a VOM to test wire media. It is probably easier to handle than a TDR.

To use a VOM, first make sure that the conductors at both ends of the cable are not touching by installing a connector on each end. Use the VOM at one end to make sure that a reading of infinity is registered on the lowest ohms scale on the meter. (On some meters, an infinity reading is indicated as an overload and is displayed as OL.) This test shows whether there are any shorts in the cable.

With the second test, you terminate one end of the coaxial cable with a connector (if this was not done already in step one), and attach a 50-ohm terminator, or short together the individual wires of each pair of the twisted-pair cable without shorting the pairs together. At the other end, you should receive a reading of slightly more than 50 ohms for coaxial cable and slightly more than 0 ohms for shorted twisted pairs. This test proves that the cable conductors have no opens.

THE INSTALLATION

Step One

The first step is to install all of the cable support hardware, including conduits and cable troughs.

Step Two

Step two is to run the cable. This sounds easy, and it can be. However, to avoid problems in later stages, follow these rules:

- Identify the cable ends with a number or letter before beginning the pull. Most electrical distributors offer kits for numbering cable ends. They contain pads of preprinted numbers that are cut so they can be wrapped around a cable. Number the end of the cable that will be pulled and then the box or roll you are pulling from.

- Avoid pulling a cable or bundling cables over a stationary cable. This will burn the stationary cable's insulation.

- Avoid using force when pulling cable. Sometimes cable bundles are heavy and a little hard to pull, but when excessive force is required, there is a problem. When you encounter heavy resistance to a pull, take the time to investigate the problem, and do not stress the cable.

- Always attach your cables out of harm's way. Cables should not be left to dangle where they may be in another contractor's way. Take the time to properly trim out the job.

• Leave a little slack. An extra foot or two at the end of each run will allow you to replace cable ends without stretching the cable if there is a problem.

Step Three

Next, install the connectors — a critical step. A bad or flaky connection will cause endless problems. The "Getting Ready for Installation" section earlier in this chapter advised you to make your team practice putting on connectors until it is proficient. This practice is tedious but essential; each connector is a link in a chain that is only as strong as its weakest link.

Step Four

The fourth step is to test each leg or segment. A TDR or VOM may be employed as described earlier in this chapter. However, TDRs are not always accurate for short cable lengths. Consult the user's guide for the TDR that you are using and use alternate testing methods for cable lengths that are shorter than the minimum length.

Step Five

Next, verify that the power in each of the equipment closets is wired properly. First use a VOM to ensure that the voltage is at the proper level. Then use an electrical wiring tester to make sure that the power is wired correctly. (See Figure 5-1.) You should consider putting an uninterruptable power source in your equipment closet to supply power to your network hardware.

Front View   Rear View

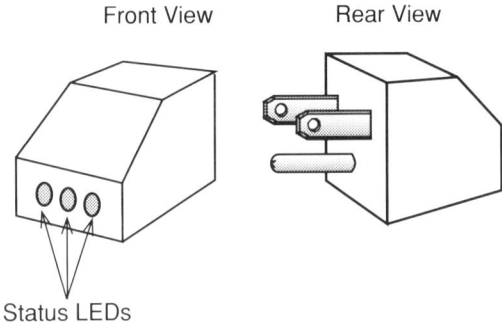

Status LEDs

Figure 5-1. Electrical Outlet Tester

When the power has been verified, install the hardware, routers, bridges, and repeaters, and run any self-tests provided for the equipment.

Step Six

You can now make the connections to the hardware. There should be no open loops, and the lines requiring termination should be properly terminated.

CASE STUDY (CONTINUED)

Back at the small investment firm, it was time to begin the installation. The network had been designed and the costs approved.

To prepare for the installation, all of the people who would be involved in it met together. The first order of business was to specify who would manage what and whom to look for with problems or questions. Then a plan for the installation was laid out, and all were assigned their initial tasks. Everyone understood what was expected.

Because some of the crew members were very experienced with the tools and techniques for installing connectors, no practice was necessary. A VOM was used to pretest all of the cable. A VOM was used because a TDR was not available. The free end of the cable was stripped back to give the VOM probes easy access. On the other end of the cable, a male BNC connector was attached to prevent the shield and center conductor from shorting. No shorts were found on any of the cables.

Next, a terminator and barrel connector were attached to the male BNC of each spool, and each roll was retested. No opens were found.

Installing Cable Support Hardware

The next task was to install all of the cable support hardware. A few D rings were installed in the beam members of the roof to attach the cable in places where no other means were available. Conduits were also installed inside every wall close to where a computer would be installed. A special outlet box called a *tiger grip box* was installed in every wall with a conduit. It was plastic and had wings that would extend and grip the drywall to hold the box in place. The backs of the boxes were cut off, and a six-inch piece of bailing wire was attached to each of the box's tops. Last, some short stubs of conduit were stubbed through the fire wall.

D-Ring Installation. Before the D rings were installed, each was wrapped with duct tape to smooth rough edges that would damage the cables. Then, a crew member on a scaffold predrilled the holes and installed the D rings.

Conduit Installation. The installation of the conduit was the most difficult part of installing the support hardware. For each location, a hole approximately two-inches square was cut in the top plate of the wall, and another hole about two by four inches high was cut directly below the first, at the bottom of the wall, 12 inches from the floor. Then, a 10-foot piece of precut, flexible plastic conduit with a one-inch diameter center was pulled down from the hole in the top plate to the top of the outlet box with a pull string.

A large nut was tied to one end of a 15-foot nylon cord to pull the conduit. One person was on a ladder, and another was on the floor next to the opening of the box. The person on the ladder dropped the end of the cord with the nut down the hole cut in the top plate. Then, the person on the floor pulled the end of the cord out of the hole made by the outlet box. The crew member on the ladder taped the cord to one end of the flexible conduit, and the one on the floor pulled the conduit down with the string. When the conduit end was in place, the tape was removed and the end was fastened to the box with the preinstalled bailing wire. The box was installed. The person on the ladder then tied down the top of the conduit with bailing wire. Tying down both ends of the conduit ensured that it would not slide into the wall or curl away from the box. These steps were repeated for every opening.

Box Installation. To prepare the wall for running the conduit, a two- by four-inch hole was cut in the drywall. When the conduit end was in place in the wall, it was tied to the box with the preinstalled bailing wire, and the box was inserted in the hole and fastened down.

Fire Wall Penetration. Where the fire wall was penetrated, three pieces of one-inch diameter, rigid metal conduit were cut to two feet and put through the wall. To do this, a 1.25- by 3.75-inch-high notch was cut on both sides of the fire wall, the lengths of conduit were slid in place, and the remaining gaps were closed with fireproof sealer. These conduits provided a permanent path for cables to run through the walls, without compromising the integrity of the fire wall.

Installing the Cable

The next step was to install the cable. The spools were placed on a rack designed for pulling cable. The loose end of each reel was marked with a unique number that was also placed on the reel. When a reel was used more than once, a new number was assigned to the cable and reel for each use.

The first bundle of cable consisted of two cables headed for the front part of the building. The next contained three cables headed for the center of the building. The last pull consisted of the last cable. The pulls were started where the multiport repeater would be installed.

Each cable pull was made through separate D rings to prevent cable burn. After the cables were pulled, the crew used tie wraps to attach them out of harm's way. Before cutting any of the cables, the crew left a minimum of 12 inches of slack at the box end and five extra feet on the end where the multiport repeater was to be installed.

Terminating Cable Ends

The members of the crew who were most experienced at installing crimp-style connectors terminated all of the cable ends. Where the ends came out of the outlet boxes, the crew used female BNC bulkhead connectors to terminate and then fastened these connectors to a plastic plate that was then screwed onto the box. At the end where the multiport repeater would be installed, the cables were terminated with male BNC connectors. Then a two-foot cable, with both ends terminated with male BNC connectors, was made for each plate.

Female BNC connectors were used in the offices to avoid using a female bulkhead barrel connector. Fewer connections entail less loss and fewer points of failure.

Testing the Segments

Next, the segments were tested with a VOM. The crew installed all of the two-foot loops on all of the plates and terminators. In the equipment room, resistance measurements were made of each line. Each line read between 51 and 53 ohms.

The Equipment Closet

In the equipment closet, where the multiport repeater was to be installed, the line voltage was tested and found acceptable. Next, a common plug tester was used to determine that the outlet was wired properly. The multiport repeater was then plugged in, and all of the segments were connected.

An Operational Network

All of the pieces were in place, and the computers were finally connected. After a little effort, all of the modifications were made to the startup files, and soon the network was declared operational.

Chapter 6

MAINTENANCE

One of the first laws of physical science is the law of entropy. Simply stated, it says that anything left to its own devices will eventually end up in chaos. This law also applies to the science of computers. A network that is not maintained and managed will become chaotic.

Management often overlooks the importance of maintaining a network. Your first task in maintaining your network is to convince management to purchase the appropriate tools.

Network maintenance is either preventative or corrective. Corrective maintenance is obviously necessary, but preventative maintenance, which is often overlooked, is equally important.

PREVENTATIVE MAINTENANCE

The network should be monitored every day, either manually or with special equipment or software. Daily monitoring helps to establish a history of network performance that enables the administrator to spot any changes. These changes may include a dramatic increase in network traffic, an increase in the error rate, or unexpected traffic patterns in off hours. They can suggest security problems, a future controller or

transceiver failure, or network overloading. By detect-
ing problems early, the administrator can manage them
proactively and possibly avoid any serious downtime or
the continuance of a security breach.

Special Equipment or Software

The two major automated ways of learning about the
health of your network are protocol analyzers and special network monitoring software. A protocol analyzer is
a computer system that attaches to the network. It
operates in what is called *promiscuous mode*, looking at
all of the packets on the network, not just those directed
to it. From the packets, the analyzer gathers information about their sources, destinations, errors, and types
of protocols used.

The information that network monitoring software
gathers depends on the package used. For example,
one manufacturer sells a monitoring package with its
hardware. This package provides information about
the loading of the network and its errors — but not on
a per-node basis, unless one of the manufacturer's
Ethernet cards is installed in each node. Without the
cards, the package cannot tell you what each node
is doing.

Manufacturer-independent monitoring software packages have started to appear on the market. Most use
the Simple Network Management Protocol (SNMP) to
gather information about the network. Because some
equipment does not use SNMP, you should check your
network before purchasing a package.

The main benefit of monitoring packages is their low price. However, the better packages may cost as much as or more than a protocol analyzer.

The protocol analyzer is usually the tool of choice, because it gathers more complete information than most software monitoring packages. The disadvantage of an analyzer is cost.

The Manual Method

This method is not very effective, though it is very simple: During the day at regular intervals, the administrator queries several network users about response time, network error messages received, and other difficulties. Users, however, are often annoyed by repeated questions, and the quality of information they provide can vary. For example, a user may view network performance differently on a rough day than on a relaxed day.

Although the manual method is not recommended, you should use it if you cannot purchase any automated tools. It is better to use a system with some inefficiencies than to do nothing and lose control of the network. Remember, the goal of this method is the same as the goal of using automated tools; that is, to spot significant changes in network performance that may indicate problems.

CORRECTIVE MAINTENANCE

Why do network components fail? Answers include hardware failure, excessive heat, power fluctuations, thermal fractures of gates, static, or just plain wear and tear. No matter the reason, once a failure occurs it must be corrected.

When there is a failure or an indication of a problem on the network, first gather as much information about the problem as possible. As an example, assume that you oversee a network comprised of thin coaxial cable. A call comes in that Joe cannot access Mary's system with the File Transfer Protocol (FTP) for file transfer. The error message from FTP is "Connection timed out" or "No response from host."

To get information about the failure, you must get a copy of the network blueprint and ask questions. From the blueprint, you can determine whether Joe and Mary are on the same Ethernet segment or re-peater. (Throughout this chapter, the term *repeater* will be used for both normal and multiport repeaters.) You can also identify all other users on the segment that Joe and Mary are on. Now you must ask ques-tions.

If Joe and Mary are on the same segment, ask the following questions:

• When was Joe's last successful FTP session with Mary? Has anything changed since then?

• In the time frame identified,

— Has any work been done on the network?

— Were any systems moved?

— Were there any accidents? (Did someone trip over a cable, for example?)

- Can Joe access his own system, from his system, through a network call such as PING?

- Can Joe access anyone else's node on the network besides Mary's?

- Can Mary access anyone else's node on the network?

- Can anyone else access Mary's node?

- Is anyone else on the segment having problems using the network?

If Joe and Mary are on different segments, ask these questions:

- When was Joe's last successful FTP session with Mary?

- Has anything changed since the last successful FTP session?

- In the time frame identified, has any work been done on the network? Were any systems moved?

- Can Joe access his system, from his own system, through a network call such as PING?

- Can Joe access anyone else's node on the network besides Mary's?

- Can Mary access anyone else's node on the network?

- Can anyone else access Mary's node?

- Is anyone else on Joe's segment experiencing difficulty with the network? Anyone on Mary's segment?

By learning when everything last appeared to be functioning properly, you can determine whether any events since then may have caused a problem. Such events include the relocation or removal of a node, a node failure, a power surge or outage, or an accident at the physical layer (for example, someone tripping over a cable).

By finding out whether Joe can access his system from his own system through a network call such as PING, you can isolate the problem node or segment. If Joe cannot access his own system in this manner, the cause of the failure is probably his connection to the segment or a segment fault.

If Joe can locally access his own node through the network but cannot reach any other nodes, your problem may involve a repeater or transceiver, a failed controller, or files improperly set up for network access (in the case of FTP, /etc/hosts, for example). Or the network may be overloaded, and the call may be timing out.

By knowing whether Mary can access other nodes, you can isolate the problem to Mary's node or segment. If anyone else on Joe's or Mary's segment is having problems, it may be the segment that has failed.

The second step is to use the information you have gathered to narrow down the source of the problem. Problems can be divided into two categories, network and nonnetwork. Network problems are related to the physical layer. They include cable, transceiver, repeater, bridge, or gateway faults. Nonnetwork problems include node failures, startup and configuration files set up incorrectly, and operator errors. The following guidelines can help you sort the problem into the proper category.

Network Problems

More often than not, if a problem involves connectivity (that is, the ability of one node to communicate with another) that was previously available, and the network has not been altered, the problem is network related. If nodes were disconnected from the network just before the problem began, the problem is probably network related. An accident, such as tripping over a cable, can also create a network problem. Problems that affect more than one node, especially when they affect a group on the same segment or repeater, point to a network problem.

Nonnetwork Problems

Problems that relate to connectivity that has been newly established but has never functioned properly are often nonnetwork related. If the network was working before some slight modifications were made to some system files (e.g., /etc/hosts on a UNIX-based system), the problem is probably related to the modifications. If a problem appears to be isolated to a single node, it is likely a nonnetwork problem.

Narrowing Down the Network Problem

If you strongly suspect you have a network-related problem, narrow down its source to a controller, transceiver, segment, repeater, cable, or other piece of hardware. You will use different techniques with each type of medium, but the concept is the same: Determine whether there is a problem with the segment or one of the cables on the segment. The first test is to ascertain the quality of the cabling connecting the nodes that have problems.

For example, with thin coaxial cable, you should first remove the BNC T connector from the back of the node and, using an ohm meter, check the resistance. Because there should be 50 ohms of termination at each end of the cable, you should see approximately 25 ohms of resistance at the T connector. The reading may fluctuate because the network is live. (See Figure 6-1.) If the reading is 50 ohms, you know that the connection to one of the terminators is no longer valid. (See Figure 6-2.)

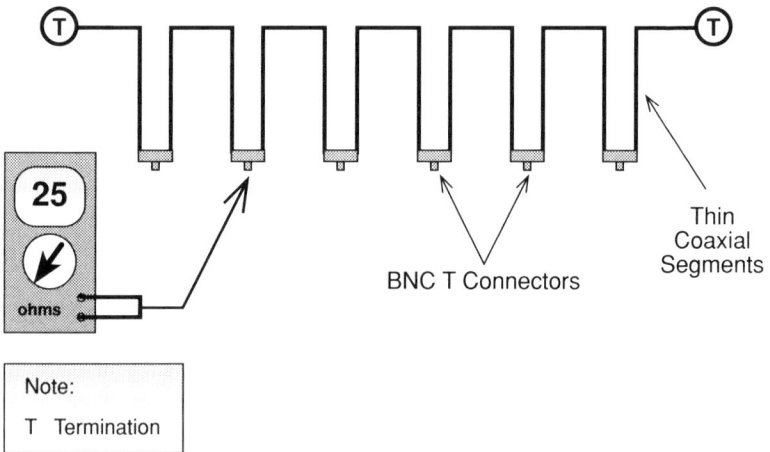

Figure 6-1. Good Measurement

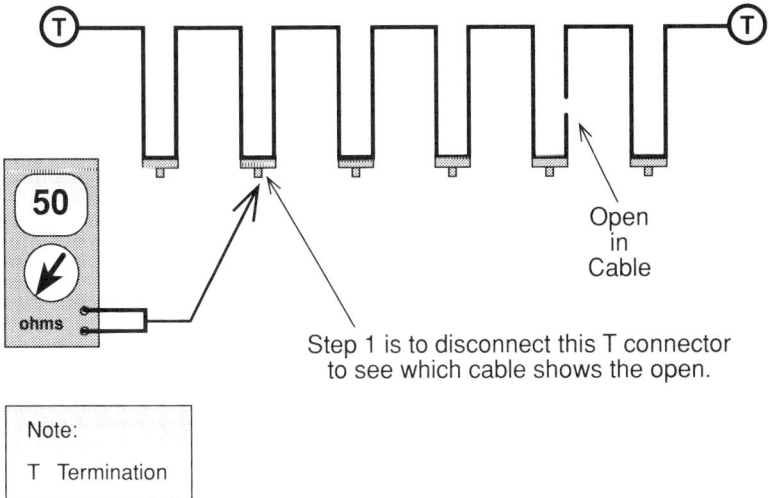

Open
in
Cable

Step 1 is to disconnect this T connector
to see which cable shows the open.

Note:

T   Termination

Figure 6-2. Missing Termination, Showing an Open

Then determine which terminator is not registering. To do this, break the connection at the T and measure each cable separately; this point will be referred to as the *start point*. Identify the cable that does not measure 50 ohms. Then use your blueprints and documentation to identify the "missing" terminator. (See Figure 6-3.)

Next, replace the T and go halfway between the start point and the "missing" terminator and remove the T; this is your new start point. Then measure each cable to determine which terminator is now missing. (See Figure 6-4.) If the same terminator is still missing, continue this cycle until you find it, and the one that you used to be able to see appears to be missing. (See Figure 6-5.)

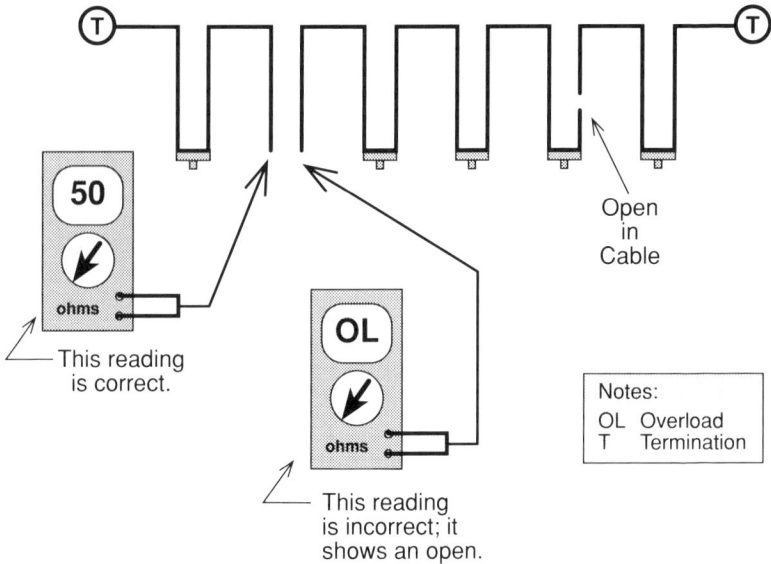

Figure 6-3. Searching for the Problem

This process is often called the *binary search method*, and it sounds a lot more complicated than it is. The concept is simple: Isolate the problem by determining where it is not. By dividing your search in half, you minimize your efforts in locating a fault.

Narrowing Down the Nonnetwork Problem

Nonnetwork-related problems depend on the operating system of the computers involved. For example, UNIX uses primarily TCP/IP protocols to communicate on a network, whereas VMS primarily uses DECnet. Each operating system and protocol has different files for controlling network activity.

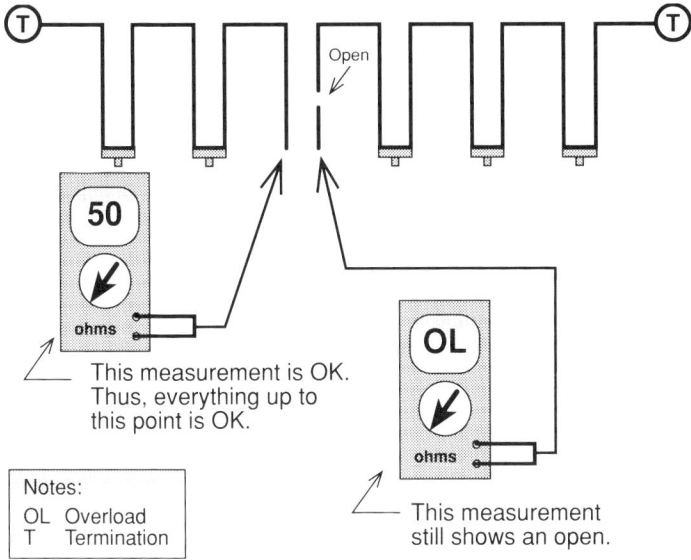

Figure 6-4. Still Searching for the Problem

The first step is to understand how your particular operating system controls the network. Identify all of the start-up and control files and what processes must run for network communication to take place. Identify how the files and processes relate to each other and their ordinal dependencies.

With this knowledge, you can start an ordered search. First, make sure the start-up files are correct, then check the control files, and last, make sure that the necessary processes are running. You should also check for security problems, such as users' accessing files or processes without permission.

TEST EQUIPMENT

A wide variety of test equipment is available for testing
network components. This equipment includes VOMs,
TDRs, network analyzers, and specialized fiber-optic
test equipment.

Selecting equipment to maintain a LAN can prove
bothersome. As you examine equipment, you may be
attracted to fancy gadgets. But, as usual, the budgets
will probably dictate that you choose only those options you need most. To make the proper selection,
thoroughly study the options available from the vari-
ous manufacturers and then think about how each
piece of equipment would work on your network. Ask
the manufacturers for demo units of the equipment
that you are most interested in.

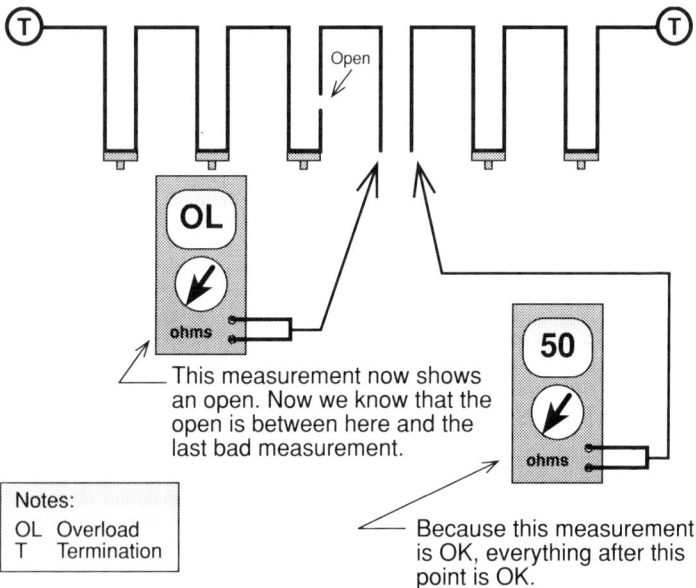

Figure 6-5. Locating the Problem

Most importantly, make sure that your equipment can be fully utilized to resolve problems on your network. There is no reason to purchase a piece of gear that tests fiber optics, for example, if you have no fiber-optic cable and do not plan to purchase any.

CONCLUSION

Troubleshooting a network is like resolving most problems. The first step is to gather all possible information about the problem. Then you start to narrow the problem down. By taking the time to understand your network topology, cabling, hardware, and system software, you will be in the best possible position to isolate and resolve your network problems quickly and effectively.

GLOSSARY

10Base-2. The IEEE 802.3-compliant implementation of Ethernet on thin coaxial cable, typically RG58/AU.

10Base-5. The IEEE 802.3-compliant implementation of Ethernet on thick coaxial cable.

10Base-T. The IEEE 802.3-compliant implementation of Ethernet on unshielded, 22- to 24-gauge twisted-pair cable.

application layer. Layer seven of the OSI model, where applications such as databases reside.

AUI cable. Attachment unit interface cable. This cable is most often used to attach such devices as workstations to transceivers. It is commonly called a drop cable.

bandwidth. **1.** A frequency range available for transmission. An AM radio has a bandwidth from 530 kHz to 1,600 kHz. **2.** A measurement of capacity. For example, the bandwidth of Ethernet is 10 Mbps; if 5 million bits of information are transmitted every second, the remaining bandwidth is 50 percent.

baseband. A transmission method in which the cable is used to transmit a single signal.

bit. Contraction of *binary digit*. This is the smallest unit of information. It may contain a value of 1 or 0.

BNC. Bayonet-locking-type connector for coaxial cable. The most common opinion is that BNC stands for Bayonet-Neill-Concelman.

bridge. A device that connects two networks using the same protocols, addressing structure, and transmission method.

broadband. The method of transmission in which a cable is used to transmit multiple signals. For example, with cable television, many channels are brought to the television on a single coaxial cable.

bus. A networking topology in which all nodes are connected to a single cable.

byte. Eight consecutive bits.

collision. An accident that occurs when two or more nodes attempt to transmit simultaneously.

CRC. Cyclic redundancy check. A method of error detection. Using a standard algorithm that performs a calculation on the packet, the transmitting station generates a number that in turn is inserted into the transmitted packet. When the receiving station receives the packet, the algorithm is applied again and the new number is compared with the transmitted number. A match indicates that the data was received as sent. A mismatch indicates a data transmission error.

CSMA/CD. Carrier Sense Multiple Access with Collision Detection. The access method that forms the basis of the IEEE 802.3 specification.

data link layer. The second layer of the OSI model. This layer establishes connections, transmits and receives data, detects errors, and releases connections.

drop cable. *See* AUI cable.

file server. A computer that provides file access to multiple users via a LAN.

frame. *See* packet.

gateway. A device that allows LANs using dissimilar protocols to be connected together. The gateway translates from one protocol to the other and handles other differences, such as data format, speed, and signal levels.

heartbeat. *See* SQE.

HVAC. Heating, ventilation, and air conditioning.

IEEE. Institute for Electrical and Electronics Engineers.

IEEE 802.3. A physical-layer standard specifying CSMA/CD on a bus topology.

jabber. Garbage that is transmitted when a node fails and continuously transmits.

LAN. Local area network. A network is said to be local when it is confined to a restricted geographical area. A LAN may have gateways to wide area networks or to other public or private LANs.

MAU. *See* media access unit.

media access unit. A transceiver. The most common application of a media access unit is running drop cables from a thick coaxial spine to individual systems; however, some transceivers convert to an AUI cable from thin coaxial, twisted-pair, and fiber-optic cable.

network layer. The third layer of the OSI model. The network layer resolves network addresses and provides service selection. This is where the Internet Protocol of TCP/IP is found.

node. Any device attached to the network, usually a computer.

packet. A set of bits, organized in a well-defined manner, for the transmission of data. The basic Ethernet packet, or frame, comprises 6 bytes for the destination, 6 bytes for the source, 2 bytes for the type or length field, 46 to 1,500 bytes for the data field, and 4 bytes for the frame check sequence.

physical layer. The first layer of the OSI model. The physical layer provides the mechanical and electrical connection and control function. The elements in this layer include the media (i.e., cabling), transceivers, and Ethernet controllers.

presentation layer. The sixth layer of the OSI model. This layer transfers information from applications to the operating system.

repeater. A device that repeats an incoming signal. The basic repeater connects two segments of Ethernet within the same LAN. It receives signals from either segment and retransmits them to both segments. The repeater also performs collision checking.

router. A device used to connect networks. Routers are able to filter packets.

RS-232. A standard recommended by the EIA for connecting data terminal equipment (DTE) and data communications equipment (DCE). RS-232 is most often referred to as a serial connection.

SQE. Signal quality error. A signal sent from transceivers to controllers to indicate an error condition. Transceivers with SQE capability cannot be used to connect repeaters to network segments. It is also called a heartbeat because when it is observed with an oscilloscope, the signal looks like it is a blip.

TDR. Time-domain reflectometer. An advanced piece of test equipment with which a user can "look" at the wire to determine its length, distance to shorts, and abnormalities.

topology. The geometric shape of a network configuration. The most common are bus, star, and ring.

VOM. Volt ohm meter. A test device used to measure the resistance, voltage, or current of a circuit.

WAN. Wide area network. A network that extends beyond the reach of LANs, covering the distance between buildings, cities, states, and countries.

X.25. A widely used communications protocol recommended by the CCITT for accessing packet-switched networks.

INDEX

D

Documentation, 29, 56, 57

Drop cable, 11

E

Ethernet

benefits, 3

definition of, 1

disadvantages, 3

transmission method, 4

packet, 7

Ethernet versions

IEEE 802.3, 8

Version 1, 8

Version 2, 8

F

Fiber-optic cable

glass fiber, 14, 16

plastic fiber, 15, 16

selection of, 39

Frame. *See* packet

G

Gateway, 25

H

Hardware. *See* network hardware

I

IEEE 802.3 standard, 8

Installation

contracting out, 50-52

contractor selection, 52-55

documentation, 56, 57

equipment closet wiring, 61

of cable, 60

of cable support hardware, 60

of connectors, 61

of network hardware, 61

management of, 52

network hardware connections, 62

preparation for, 58

scope of the project, 50-52

stages, 49

TDR test, 58

testing of segments, 61

VOM test, 59

ISO, 1

M

Maintenance

corrective, 69, 71

preventative, 69, 70

manual method, 71

special equipment or software, 70, 71

Media. *See* cabling

Multiple access, 4

Multiport repeater, 21, 22

N

Network design

cable connector selection, 39

cable route plans, 41-43

documentation, 29

hardware selection, 44

media selection, 37-39

network traffic analysis, 34, 35, 36

rules for, 27-32

usage characteristics, 32

Network hardware

bridge, 23, 24

O

P

R

Repeater, 21, 32

Router, 24

S

Session layer, 2

SNMP, 70

T

Tap

 inline, 15

 invasive, 15

 noninvasive, 15

TDR, 58

Testing

 of segments, 61

 with a TDR, 58, 59

 with a VOM, 59

Thick coaxial cable, 13, 15, 39

Thin coaxial cable, 17, 38

Thinnet, 17

Token Ring, 25

Transceiver, 19

Transport layer, 2

Troubleshooting, 71-81

Twisted-pair cable, 17, 18, 38

V

VOM, 59